Contents

The *nom de plume*	1
Acknowledgements	2
Introduction	4
Chapter 1	
My options	10
Chapter 2	
Training	23
Chapter 3	
Apartheid	36
Chapter 4	
Dwaalboom	44
Chapter 5	
Accommodation	54
Chapter 6	
Work	65
Chapter 7	
Long weekends	83

Chapter 8

Boredom 99

Chapter 9

The *Happening* that couldn't happen 109

Chapter 10

10 – 0 127

Afterword 135

Joe Britton

The *nom de plume*

The author is a man of very many years of a life, that have been full of dramas mostly of other people's makings, generally taking a back seat, yet knowing all whilst, that this seat, is not a seat that should be sat in by anyone.

A most unremarkable man who has, as so many men have in their lives, lived it in quiet desperation, with the sole aim of getting to the finish line. But before doing so, wanting to do something that is positive and can be of benefit to others, indeed that is the primary purpose of life. Not to leave it as you have found, and simply switch out the lights before you go out, but to depart having made it a better place, be it big or be it small, that is but all we are compelled to do and, on that basis, this tale is told from a moment in his life in 1984 when there was no big brother watching and neither was it on tv..

Acknowledgements

To the people written about here, especially to Victor, a man who was so cool I tried to be like him after meeting him.

To the men who could see beyond the stars and made it happen when it wasn't allowed.

To Isaac and the look in his eye, a look of certainty, in the certainty that Apartheid would be no more.

Donny who remained a friend for a little while with the power of communication via snailmail which ended as all such correspondences usually do. A friendship at the time that sustained me through this period with his good humour and zest for life. The time I asked him why he drank so much one weekend and he stopped to pause for a second, have a drag on his cigarette and ponder the question by replying 'because I like it'. He said it with such clarity that I thought this man is a sage!

Down to my final weekend there when I was to go into a jeweller's to buy a gift, with him persuading me not to, as I would run out of beer money. I don't believe he had ever been a boy scout, but with such foresight, he surely could have been.

Also, my dear friend Tomasz C whom I have known for only twenty years. It's funny as you get older, that expression 'for only' actually makes sense. It was only in very recent times that he decided to come clean and advise me that all the stories I would tell him, that he found them to be rather boring but thought this one could be made into a book and pushed me into doing so...

Introduction

Grimsby, I have been told is a Viking port, simply because places ending in BY suggests this.

What I've found out in the intervening years through the power that is the internet, is Grimsby is a port town in Lincolnshire, England.

Grimsby joins the town of Cleethorpes forming a conurbation. It also is the home of a famous bridge, the Humber bridge which has a span approximately a mile long to link North Lincolnshire to the East Ridings of Yorkshire, it was once the longest single span bridge in the world. I have heard this phrase 'The bridge from out to nowt'! This is unfair as indigenous people everywhere tend to love where there from. In fairness to this bridge, it has saved millions of hours of valuable travel time and to that end reduced emissions. It is a grade I listed landmark made so within the last ten years by Historic England due to its state-of-the-art engineering design. It is 72km north-east of Lincoln and some 53km via the Humber Bridge to the south-east East Ridings of Yorkshire.

I have always visualized it as a sparsely populated region and that it was also fishing town, I got this information from generally just growing up. I now know It has a population of about 85,000 people. Grimsby has notable landmarks including Grimsby Minster, Port of Grimsby, Cleethorpes Beach and Grimsby Fishing Heritage Centre. Grimsby was once the home port for the world's largest fishing fleet around the mid-twentieth century, but fishing as we all know has fell dramatically. Those of a certain generation could not forget the Cod Wars denying UK access to Icelandic fishing grounds and the EEC used its Common Fisheries Policy to parcel out fishing quotas to other European countries in waters within 370km of the UK coast.

Grimsby people are called Grimbarians; also, Cod-heads which is used jokingly, often for football supporters. Great Grimsby Day is 22nd January. This port town is the second largest settlement by population in Lincolnshire after Lincoln. However, to this day I have never been there.

At an evening talk, in more recent times given by a learned society branch of a certain institution regarding the bridge, it was found that the steel bearing supports at each end had seized over time and as such required immediate repair. It wasn't helped by haulier's and the like, pressurizing their wheels to reduce the surface contact with the deck, to reduce tyre wear, but in doing so increase the point loads on the bridge seriously damaging the deck which wasn't designed for such loading.

The local authority conducted this routine inspection of the bearings at the tower supports in 2020 and in their findings, they discovered that the bearings in the supports had failed, as they were seized up. In many ways due to Covid 19, this presented the perfect opportunity to repair these supports, not in a way to compromise the bridge but rather to introduce new bearings and once this work was complete, decommission the existing ones. by making them redundant. Happy days with only one day lost for crossings due to the low traffic usage, meant that half the deck could be closed and repaired and the other half could remain open, done in a sequencing manner. Covid 19 has a lot to answer for but in this case was immensely beneficial.

Back to the tale ... many many years ago I was an undergraduate studying for a degree in Civil Engineering, the course I took was a sandwich course not of the food variety, but comprised an overall four year period which included the 'sandwich' element of two; six month periods of work experience within these four years, so you can imagine companies wouldn't really be too interested in a non-qualified person to be put on a payroll with their company and, probably the hardest part of doing the degree course was getting the correct or sufficient work experience required to continue, to obtaining a degree. So, for each year of year two and year three, there was the arduous task of scouting round with the help of the college to get a placement for these two time periods. In year three, I got two offers of work experience, which was very uncommon. These options given to me were either to work for a contractor on a building site in Grimsby doing setting out duties, that, being: To provide lines and levels in order to construct the building within building tolerances, a nice enough prospect, the work that is, but I wasn't so sure about Grimsby for some reason, my other offer was to work in South Africa during the Apartheid era. I recall thinking of the former and then the latter and going hmm... I've heard of this Grimsby, sounds a bit grim, it's on the east coast of England and I've never heard that much about it, I'm not sure they have a football team, notwithstanding the aforementioned desk study to confirm they do! And on that basis, I think I would prefer to go somewhere else being South Africa. No disrespects to Grimsby of course, but I thought this must be a more appealing place than Grimsby. As previous under graduates had gone to South Africa from this college, with tales of adventures such as living in places like Port Elizabeth and Durban, that sounded great to me, one had told me of a place called Swaziland, and what it had to offer. When pressing initially to what location we would be sent, the answer from the Placement Officer in the college was, you will only know when you get there. It will be where you are needed or where they can accommodate such inexperienced personnel. So that was the choices, and with my simple thought process I decided on South Africa, thinking about the likes of Durban which had a beach. This placement was also with a building contractor, I think the college preferred we went on site, so as to allow us to put our building design and theory into practice once we had graduated.

In many ways it was a toss up as to where to go, however South Africa sounded the best option simply due to the weather and also never having travelled outside of the UK before, so that was the simple thought process in opting for South Africa. No more or no less, and being of a young mind, with no access then to internet and such like to convince me otherwise.

Most of the of the above, I knew nothing of. It can be said that one's early years, it takes about ten years from the cradle, to shape what a person will ultimately become, with their traits now formed and which act as a benchmark throughout life and it is why it is so important to provide nurture to combat nature, nature of course is something innate and binding, however nurturing of a young person is vital to what they are to become, so faced with a moral issue of the latter placement location at an age when I should have known better, posed a moral issue to be addressed. However, by the time you are a young adult our belief systems are well established. What comes after is a wrestle with these and other factors that may compromise them, such as survival, ambition or a means to an end. This book is merely a tale of a means to an end and as with all choice's life has on offer at various times there are so many paths to go down, we hardly know which one is the right one. Looking back almost every person, I think would have taken a different path, the path I took was mine and mine alone so without further *adieu* I will regale what this option I took in terms of job experience, this being the requisite to completing my degree.

Chapter 1

My options

In 1984 Apartheid was barely known to me as a system, nor did I know it was in the death throes of coming to an end, although the latter was not obvious at the time. Aided to its rightful demise were sanctions placed on the Republic of South Africa, driven primarily by the US, the irony of this is this being that this is a country that was formed in essence upon similar lines, to now being widely accepted as the so called worlds police force, but why? Nobody asked them to be.

This sanctioning and sermonizing driven primarily by the US was treated with distain by the white population only of South Africa. When I look back, and on looking back it is easy to see why they thought like this, as the alternative could have been obliteration and wipe out, much like that had happened in other African countries after foreign rule, upon hand over, or even like what happened to the small white population by that evil nut Mugabe in neighboring Zimbabwe, the people there are not free, they are trapped in financial straits and subjugated still by the dictators that followed and are to this day, but hey, what country isn't in ways we probably will never find out, of course two wrongs don't make a right and the Apartheid system had to go as no one should be classified by the colour of their skin. The argument at the time was when the Boer's arrived they claimed it was *bantu* land ie The Cape uninhabited and set about carving out a large tranche of land for themselves, in easy to fit provincial boundaries, mainly straight lines, ironically like they are in America.

It was *so 'bantu'* that the Boer's got many a local woman pregnant and the offspring were, in the latter to be formed Apartheid system, classified as coloured aka the cape coloured's, as opposed to black being lower down the hierarchy of Apartheid, white, coloured and black, incidentally the white race group comprised four classes described in Chapter 3.

So, what was I to do as a student in 1984? Doing a degree which involves two, six-month stints of work experience as part of the curriculum? One of our lecturers was a South African of the white persuasion and had set up an affiliation with a South African construction company whom he had prior to worked for and got agreement for the placement of six students per work term to gain experience on site.

The irony, if there is such a one, is our class was the last class to undertake this *opportunity*, because the Student Union, thereafter, banned this work experience outlet on the grounds that it was overt racism which of course it was.

For myself as previously stated I was offered a placement in Grimsby or South Africa. now again, no disrespects to Grimsby, this must be understood! I started to feel excited at the thought of South Africa. The thought grew on me.

But when I started to read about Apartheid, I promised myself I would not abuse or show disrespect to anyone by going there. It seemed like an adventure that was not to be turned down, what with free flights, accommodation and food! Plus, the chance to see the world, that was the offer I took up in the mid 1980's.

With our budget getting there was to be done by the cheapest way possible, meaning many different flights to various destinations on the way, with hours of waiting between each stoppage until the next flight, this only exacerbated our drunkenness on a student scale. At one airport, we queued up at the wrong departure gate, but the ground staff had kept an eye on us and directed us to the appropriate gate. I'm sure this was done not out of professionalism but the desire to get rid of us out of their airport and out of their responsibility. In reality we have to be thankful they were there as otherwise so would we!

The Republic of South Africa was formed essentially as a white nation, with huge swathes of indigenous people flocking to the 'modernized' region looking for work, so much so the authorities felt if they didn't act, there would be no new country of theirs anymore, so came up with this Apartheid plan, because after all, if it *wasn't* for the white man, there wouldn't be South Africa unless they discovered the diamonds in the diamond mines of Kimberly, that were constructed thereafter! This idealistic (for whites), way of life, must sustained and *voila* Apartheid!

I am a bit of a dreamer I suppose and there are quite a lot of people in their younger years who experience *de ja vu*, but as one grows older these types of occurrences diminish. I have been prone to such experiences, but this one was not such an experience. It was a dream, a dream of Johannesburg, that I dreamt of as a child, to such an extent I somehow knew where it was, so looked it up on a map and found the name of this place. As I was pondering Grimsby and overseas, I thought of this and thought it must have meant something and it would be a lie to suggest this made my mind up but it certainly added a few percentage points to my decision. In this dream I had seen streets, paved with gold as a direct reference to the wealth of minerals and precious metals that this part of Africa is blessed with.

I had only ever lived in and had never left the British Isles up to that point, I had also heard of the expression ex pat and had wondered what that was, so I found out that it was a term used for people who worked and lived overseas to a higher standard of living than they would have had if they had stayed at home. I had to have a bit of that to feel this experience.

I remember tv programmes and sometimes people talking about jet lag as some sort of badge of honour, I thought to myself I also want to have a piece of that!

Then I thought of the weather, sunshine or constant drabness of Grimsby, granted it was a summer period for this work placement, but I had been fooled all my life about summer and sunshine! So sunshine, a feeling of being warm, experiencing a new way of living, not really understanding what implications it would have on me as a person, if any, but it did mean a guarantee of new adventures of a kind I would never have again and different people and culture, so it did appeal to my wanderlust and I simply wanted to go and didn't turn down this offer.

I had seen on tv, that Zimbabwe was on the news and how it had obtained its freedom, so at the time Southern Africa was a topic being covered. It would be a completely be remiss of me to write that there was much of a decision to be made, it was South Africa for me. At this juncture I failed to mention one of the other main reasons for wanting to go, that being perhaps meeting a Blonde ridiculously good looking woman who would fall in love with a foreign accent and by chance not notice how out of her league I would be because she would put my awkwardness as well as silliness to merely down to the charming traits of a standard foreigner, although this theory was quickly debunked.

Once this decision was made it was simply a matter of informing the Careers Officer within the college to register for this 'adventure' bearing in mind the decision needed to be made pretty jack smart due to the limited places available. As it happens not all the allocations were taken up, only five of us took up these placements. I put this down to some students bottling it, not aware in truth it could have been of a conscientious nature of the others but I somehow doubt it, as it was a big decision especially before the global village concept was a reality.

So, prior to setting off, all that was left for me to do was exit myself from my rented accommodation and return home for a week or so to re charge the batteries and if possible, find out a little more about South Africa, but this was a very limited research task as nobody I knew had ever been there!

It was by quite chance I was in a public house and was speaking to a guy who just so happened to be the brother of an ex-girlfriend, she adored him and would tell me he was overseas and working in Ghana. I think with most ex pats all they want to do when its holiday time is to go home for this period, this was the Case with him. I was at an advantage to him as I knew off him and spoke briefly about his sister before asking him what it was like living and working in Africa. As it was The Eighties it was normal to receive around Christmas time from contractors such things as alcoholic spirits or nudie calendars, but this guy didn't get this sort of Christmas Gift off the contractor he was working with on site as a Resident Engineer. Instead, he told me he received a knock on his office door the previous Christmas time and upon opening it, a young woman presented herself to him courtesy of the contractor as his Christmas Gift! Which he told me that he politely declined, so I must take him at his word.

Back to the travelling; we firstly had to hire a car to get to Heathrow. As I have noted, all that went was a party of five and it became my task to hire a car and shell out the money. To this day one of these lads still Owes me £18 and I still want it! He was a Welsh lad but he had the personality of a shoe and his name is long forgotten to me and besides when writing such a tome one can easily be sued!

The journey started in the hire car with myself picking it up and collecting the party outside the college and proceeding down to Heathrow on the motorway, I had never been on a Motorway in my life and making things more challenging, we had no real idea where it was! But somehow with a Road Map and a lad in the car kind of knowing which way it was, it seemed to me that every destination you ever wanted to go, was always positioned in the centre of the road map page and difficult to look for, as was the case with Heathrow.

The five of us eventually Got to Heathrow, I felt the pressure of the responsibility of driving my fellow students safely to the airport, because this nit who still owes me the money was sat in the middle of the back seat meaning I couldn't use this window to look at the rear of the car for traffic as all I saw every now and then was him living and breathing my drive non stop, with on occasion some negative comment about my driving which to be fair I was not the *May West*.

Heathrow was huge, but one of the lads had been there before and somehow like a herd of cattle we followed him to the check-in desks. I remember thinking to myself all these people, yes, *all* these people seem to know where they are going, when myself had not a clue! I do not recall what happened to the hire car as to the drop off point, save to say we got there in one piece and *Havis* simply had a quick inspection of the car and we were good to go.

After check in was drink in, at the time drinking at each and every turn made no sense to me. I later got wise, but really got unwise to this concept, (but that's Not for here). So, we proceeded to get stupefied as it was such an exciting and in ways a scary time, the thoughts of travelling beyond the equator that had been a staple of my life.

As with all urban myths we were told such things as the constellations on the other side of the equator are almost identical to the Northern Hemisphere, to this day I have never bothered to either confirm or refute this, the other one which may be true is that water when draining in a sink swirls in the opposite direction in the Southern Hemisphere, again I cannot say whether this is true on an experimental level as I don't know which way it swirls down a sink now, even if I did I would have to constantly have to conduct this high tech experiment to make it stay in my memory.

The reasons for going outweighed the reasons not to go, I was never challenged on the matter anyway by going on such an adventure that was morally wrong. I know full well now, that in my youth I had the morals of a rabbit and to sit and think about such matters never entered my head, to me it was a means to an end. I do remember one of our students being advised not to go as this student was indeed from Africa and I do remember him leaving the lecture room at this. This incident didn't stir any sense of doing anything in me, but a feeling of sadness as seeing his distress, luckily, he had the fortitude to continue his studies. This was the eighties and empathy was in Short Supply. I would like to think it was due to no enlightenment or any sense of awareness, which for me it most certainly was. I had seen plenty of racism in my life and in my ignorance thought nothing of it. I had never stopped to think of standing in other people's shoes until many many years later.

I think it was at this stage the realization of the option of going overseas instead of a simple train journey struck, and all of a sudden the more correct option to have adopted should have been Grimsby, but by then, it was too late, the grass is always greener as they say. I cannot corroborate this, but only surmise it would have been Grimsby that would have won that, even though I still haven't gone there, but certainly in South Africa as I found out, it was never green.

Chapter 2

Training

We arrived somehow to South Africa. Now as we were to be 'supervisors' on site, simply because as we weren't experienced enough to do any real work as we were students with no real knowledge of construction.

As we had been treated on arrival to being lodged in a very reputable hotel. When the companies representatives arrived to inform us we had to travel to a training school, we had by then somehow developed a sense of entitlement. They had laid out a single hire car for us to travel to the camp, but we collectively argued that there was not enough leg room in such a car for five and convinced them that we required two cars, which were duly presented to us, what were they to do with these 'militants', after spending all that money on us to get there, simply send us back? I don't think so, they might get some value out of us after all, although that certainly wasn't the case. As I really don't think any of us went to work but simply to gain a new experience and have a holiday!

We had to go to this training camp before we could be sent to the various sites the construction company had, so, we needed to know a little about construction techniques, learn about reinforced concrete, as well as how to align metal shutters, to understand the dangers of hydrostatic head during pouring of wet concrete and the need for adequate bracing of the formwork prior to concrete placing, which in essence means learning both to create the form and also deal with the water pressure of concrete being poured in its liquid state, we were also taught heavens knows why, how to steel fix ie tie reinforcement together with tying wire with pinchers.

Our teacher was a classy man, a black man who was known as N'Jebba (this is phonetic) and in Zulu means 'bearded one'. He had a fine beard! In passing, months later, he was placed the site I was assigned to in his capacity as a charge hand to lead a gang of workers. All construction work was generally done or rather most physical work was done by the black people. I recall one day him seeing me, it was a huge site.

It was a cement works at the locus of the enormous gypsum seam, which was constructed on a grand scale as there was so much land that they built the plant where it was needed and provided new infrastructure to support it, such as new railway lines to service the transport of this raw material, they also would construct a new village area in and around Dwaalboom for the workers of the cement works.

N'Jebba, when on site, would always address me 'hello bosse'! I remember feeling a little embarrassed knowing how good he was as a teacher and such a leader of men. I later found out at this stage of Apartheid, he was just playing the game of white supremacy, with subtly younger people being addressed as bosse as opposed boss. I do recall one incident many months later, being called 'Master' by an older man and also recall the shocked looks on the black people around him by him addressing me in this subservient way, for my part it was it was not shock, but embarrassment and a sense of sadness that a fellow human, had got used to addressing people like that.

Anyway, the training was a two week course attending a construction school, to design falseworks and discuss construction, which at that time had no emphasis on site safety, simply on construction, these classes followed practical lessons of erecting steel shutters as well as tying together reinforcement. I recall getting a blister on my finger from using tying wire. It was sore for a few days but thought it was just a blister, as I'd never done any real physical work and it would eventually heal; but it simply wouldn't heal as we did this task a number of times thereafter and eventually it went septic, so I was driven to a hospital and seen straight away to have minor surgery to get the finger lanced. I recall getting the best of attention of both the doctor and nurses which thankfully saved my digit to do other things, like write this!

The Welsh guy in our group, took this training very seriously and would generally be at the training camp a good fifteen to twenty minutes before our tasks began, be it practical or theoretical. I remember thinking what a weird guy this bloke was, as he kept to himself at night, (each to their own), when eventually we departed going our separate ways to the various parts of South Africa.

The £18 he Owed me remained still Owed. I don't know why I never asked it off him as I presumed, he would honour his debt, which he never did, and besides he was weird anyway! He was the first ever person whomever fitted the description not yet coined at that time of a *Billy no mates*. What disturbed me however was, we looked in appearance similar and sometimes I would be called by his name! thankfully I remember his name not, but still want my £18!

The practical tasks were the worst, after we had spent time in a classroom designing formwork, we would be broken up into groups to perform the formwork techniques to form the various moulds we had designed, they were all very rudimentary. In the UK and most elsewhere, formwork in those days was plywood which had a life cycle of two to perhaps four re-uses before being discarded for new plywood. In South Africa, the formwork was modular steel panels, the smallest easily being 20kg in weight, but the re-use of this type of shuttering was limitless and besides it was black workers who had to do the work so what did it matter if the work was tough on them that was what I thought was the reasons anyway.

On the days of doing the practical work, these days for us were pretty tiring, and part of the task was to dismantle it all this being done against the clock for speed and accuracy, I guess to give us a sense of what the workers should and could be capable of which would have been a darn site more than us.

Some of the more inventive of us noticed the supervisor would migrate away from his office and attend to the various people doing these practical tasks, and they would nonchalantly enter his office to make use of the facilities, by using the phone, which had no restrictions on international calls, which meant for two weeks it would be reasonable to assume after our stint there, that the phone bill would be substantial indeed.

Evenings were spent in a large single storey building nearby occupied by white people sent there for various training such as refresher courses. The people serving, provided food and laundry services. They also stayed on site but slept in another building at night. The white South Africans of the Dutch persuasion ie the Afrikaners were known by other whites as *rock spiders*, or *yarpies*, simply as they were perceived as incredibly boring which I also found them to be, I preferred *rock spider* as they were pretty dry too.

Television was a non starter as it had perhaps, only three channels mostly all in Afrikaans, although on some occasions it would break out and show an odd Sporting or American Series or film sub-titled in Afrikaans, so this meant every night the older guys would drink an entire bottle of spirits whilst playing either darts or cards, with us penniless students watching on for our 'fun' until we took up playing cards.

On some late afternoons after training camp we would venture out to the rock hard fields adjoining the accommodation and attempt to play a bit of football, but having no boots, not that you needed them as the ground was rock hard and grassless, so grip was not an issue.

Playing this type of football quickly lost its charm. The evenings were strange as there was no such thing as twilight as we knew it, here sunset arrived by being one moment light, the next it was dark.

There was no chance amongst the more adventurous of us to break out so to speak and go to a liquor store, this was for two very good reasons, no money nor transport.

It has to be said that the food provided for us although of course different in taste and indeed type was made very well and was quite wholesome and for us, much needed as none of us I believe had ever did a day's work in our lives and the 'practical's', were extremely grueling as they were done and required to be done in full length work overalls and helmets that had to be worn at all times, which meant we were constantly boiling hot, but never had any sweat to show for it, simply because it evaporated upon release onto our skin.

One of the candidates at the training camp was a white Rhodesian, he was as young as ourselves, being in his early twenty's, he was a fine looking young man, although he was of the habit of all the other rock spiders of consuming a bottle of spirits each night, which was considered completely normal.

This man, was using crutches to play darts, as one of his legs was missing, which he told us when we got to know him was from the civil war in his country, he told us of all the goings on there and was both shocked and annoyed at how little we knew of the political unrest in his country from the narrative given to us in the UK. As we all know the news is very selective on all matters. It was out of that political unrest that numerous white Rhodesians as they were called, had emigrated to South Africa where they were taken in with open arms.

These two weeks over the course of the six months seemed to be the longest part of our stay, partly due to it being a new environment and having no fixed base and having to actually do something. Other factors would have been mild culture shock as well as the first experiences of Apartheid, which in this particular place was not particularly overt, but clear in the sense that other candidates at this training camp stayed in different accommodation along race lines and all the people doing the menial works in and around the accommodation were all black people.

Sleeping quarters were not too bad, it was I think around four beds to a room dormitory with fresh bedding every day, there was never a chance of oversleeping due to the heat and bright light in the morning and I suppose our youth, with a hearty breakfast supplied prior to walking yes walking! To and from the accommodation to the training school per day. We didn't receive meals at the training camp, but were supplied with carry outs of food which I think was known as mealy pop, it appeared rice based, but tasted different to what I was used to, and generally non of us took to it, but that wasn't a problem as we needed it for nourishment to do the tasks we were doing.

The heat and aridness of the place, and the training work we did in the practical lessons was enough for me, quite how the workers, I was to go on site to supervise did this physical work for a full shift was beyond me, one of my tasks later on was to speak to workers to keep moving if somebody slowed down, what kind of a job was that? I was also amazed how little was thought of the black people, yet almost to a single person they were multi-lingual, able to speak of course their own tongue but also Afrikaans *and* English, not just pidgin English but properly articulated.

It occurred to me how all the different tribes could speak to each other although different languages, I was told they used something (phonetically) called *fannygalore,* a bit like Esperanto which thankfully never took off, so they could all communicate throughout South Africa using this, the actual name to this language is *Fanagalo*, based primarily on Zulu with input from English and a small amounts of Afrikaans. Used mainly on construction sites, in the gold, diamond, coal and copper mining industries in South Africa and to a lesser extent in other countries like The Congo, Zambia and Zimbabwe. I am told since South Africa won its independence it is not so much spoken now as English is a common tongue.

When it was time to go from the training school, I know for sure we were all beyond pleased it was time to go, we were given two hired cars again, to drive to Johannesburg to stay in an hotel again for the weekend, once again the obligatory blow out on booze, as if it was about to run out, some locals in the hotel told us they drank as their wasn't much else to do in the country except drink. So, we drank non- stop until the following Monday.

One of those nights we all went to a nightclub, of an underground variety, simply because there where hardly any bars to speak of. This club was a gay club and you had to be gay to get in, but it was the only one open we could find, for me being as thin as a rake, unable to grow a beard, my main problem was not looking gay, but to get in at all, I was twenty two at the time and had to take my passport with me everywhere I went that sold alcohol. My abiding memory is of the male toilets that had no boundary for the women in the place to enter. My other memory is watching an old man slow dancing a younger man in tight white corduroys, but for me the worst part was watching at the bar two men French kissing each other while they stayed on their bar stools, only for the man in the middle turning to his other side and passionately kiss another bloke, it was both to me an eye opener and gave me a sick feeling.

Once the weekend ended the representatives of our new company allocated us in a random way to various sites that they had throughout the republic. We bid farewell to each other as we departed to these different sites to work on, for my sins I was allocated a site in the Northern Transvaal to a place called Dwaalboom.

This place could have been called Timbuktu for all I cared as I had never heard of this place, but what a journey to get there, lasting more hours than I thought possible, looking out onto a landscape of sandy flat land and the odd modern town interspersed with townships were from my vantage point provided for only the basic needs such as a water pump, I remember observing.

Upon arrival, I discovered the accommodation comprised three camps which were called huts, segregated as one for white, one for coloured and one for black workers.

To go to site in the mornings we would be transported there by a shuttle bus, this was also afforded to the coloured camp, but for the black camp, the workers, were to make their own way by walking to site. The black camp, was strategically placed well, as it was the closest of the camps to the building site but a fair distance non the less.

Chapter 3

Apartheid

I can only speak of Apartheid from the perspective of my own personal experience, I do not wish to be an authority on it as not only am I not interested in such a concept, I simply do not want to give it any credence of justification but merely to report how I found it and my understandings of it correct or otherwise and my thoughts on how it came to pass.

It is beyond comprehension to think that judgement can be made on anyone because of colour. I mean I was born white; someone who was born another colour didn't ask to be just as I didn't. Who is to say what the superior colour is? The answer is simple, there is no such thing, 'we are all God's children', this quote was a quote from a man I worked with called Isaac who was a Cape Coloured by race as it was known to be at the time.

The White Race Group, comprises four classes in order of hierarchy that the regime decreed.

- First spoken language Afrikaans
- First spoken language English/ other language
- White immigrant any language
- Japanese

The Coloured Race Group

- Asian
- Chinese
- Half caste (white/black)

The Black Race Group

- Indigenous or non-indigenous

Whilst working on a construction site I noticed all the white personnel were all called boss, it didn't matter their role, such as site agent, lead surveyor, they were always addressed 'boss' by the black workers, however to the coloured race, there was more parity of esteem and they didn't have to address people by such words as 'boss'.

I was told under no circumstances to allow any of the black workers address me by my first name as this was considered taboo and indeed some of these workers noticed my naivety and some would invariably call me by my first name, I was told 'just now they will lose respect', so I knew I couldn't allow this, which was difficult but I knew also, why they were doing it and why not, however I felt paradoxically I was being insulted and had on occasion told the workers not to call me by my given name.

Asians in general assisted the white personnel in non-physical work roles such as foremen to give site orders, it felt to me that the black workers preferred this, but that is only an observation.

Asians didn't get it that easy with the whites and in times of argument or making derogatory remarks they could be known as 'coolies', I think we all know that black people in such situations would be remarked as being k-----s, a term we all know to be abhorrent. I found the Asians in their own subliminal way would have their own private clubs, and made it mandatory that if you as a white were to accompany an Asian to their club, you would always be made to 'sign in', it was their way I suppose to have a pop back at the whites.

It was not unknown for some integration between white and Asian were on occasion one could be invited to dine with an Asian, which for some reason made the latter perceive themselves of having a better social standing all of this is nonsense of course but normalised somehow by the regime.

Coloured people would also in general take up none physical jobs, such as surveying or being made charge hands, and depending on their skill set could be allowed to become foremen.

However, as stated it was only the preserve of the whites to be called boss, Asians and Coloured were called by their given name if they so wished so it was a hierarchy within a hierarchy of complexities beyond my knowledge or interest.

Black people were the physical workers, in all forms of construction, the work was labour intensive, and work had to be done in an overzealous standard not required in construction, for instance, when digging foundations, prior to placing cement based blinding to receive reinforced concrete foundations, they were made to brush the specks of dirt prior to placing the concrete blinding, a completely useless element of work.

As noted previously, all formwork was steel panels with flanges to allow modular formwork, placed to exacting lines and levels not required for construction below ground level, the work must have been exhausting having to use these heavy forms of shuttering, but hey it was cost affective, so that's all that mattered, certainly not the workers wellbeing.

It was said and it was certainly true from my observations of a number of foreign white nationals on the site, that white immigrants could be 'the worst' in terms of bossing people about as to have this new superior complex over their fellow man, these in particular had little understanding of Apartheid and were generally could order workers to do the most menial work and call them names for which you would be rightly arrested for now, such tasks ordered by ordering them off site to wash their cars or clean other things of that nature. By comparison the white South Africans tended to give orders in a more orderly sensible manner, but certainly done without empathy.

The language Afrikaans is a Dutch dialect but given a title that appeared as if it was some form of indigenous language, but of course it isn't.

I remember once going into a shop to buy something, and in front of me waiting in line were two black people, the shop keeper simply looked over their heads and asked me what I wanted, and I duly did my shop. I do remember at the time feeling a little odd at being part of this, I also remember feeling that this was normal, yes I was now buying into Apartheid as it suited me, I didn't feel shame at my behaviour I had simply acclimatised to the status quo.

I did a few other things in this manner of behaviour which I regret, I can only apologise to by perhaps, by recalling this here for the record.

We had somehow in our last week got the week off before flying back home, the chance to go to a beach quite a drive and a '*jol*' (an Afrikaans term that migrated into English speakers as well as other words).

When we got to the beach, this took ages due to the vastness of the country. I saw a notice at the entrance to the beach The notice read: 'This beach is reserved solely for the white race group'. I thereafter found out only these beaches had shark nets, I also remember a black man on this beach there, he was not a normal sized black man, but a man with a physique which suggested he was from overseas, he most certainly wasn't asked to leave the beach by the lifeguards!

The well trotted out line by the Boers was that it was their country, and it was not for outsiders to interfere in what they had built, and it was their right to this land that they had built up from open planes, there was no mention of the peoples they replaced.

As mentioned previously, but not apparent at the time Apartheid was coming to an end, it was I was told when there, that it was a much watered down version of Apartheid, I'm glad I wasn't there earlier if that was the case. However, on reflection I can understand what they must have meant. Because the building site I was on, I would think the majority of the work force hailed from the neighbouring country above South Africa to the north, Botswana and it did occur to me at the time, was Apartheid was so bad, that people from another country were prepared to work there as economic migrants? The reality is that it wasn't that this regime was not so bad, the reality was these workers were simply economic migrants, that due to their financial circumstances, were impelled to go to another country under a system based on race. It meant they unfortunately had to play along with this repressive system, because of better wages or simply to get work, this was the price they were prepared to play so to speak, that price was *Apartheid*, which meant living in segregation and calling a white man boss, but you didn't have to mean it.

Chapter 4

Dwaalboom

Upon landing in Johannesburg that night of arrival and looking out of the window it was amazing to see all these cars driving on freeways to and from places I didn't really think existed, this was a big country and plenty of motorways, it struck me as exiting and surreal. Although I was in for a shock when going to Dwaalboom.

Dwaalboom is an Afrikaans word for loan tree, and a short time after getting there when away from site or lodgings, better known as the white hut, described in Chapter 5. I took a ride to Dwaalboom and seen very few houses but did see a crossroad and also the lone tree on which this 'town' was named after.

My abiding memory of that visit to Dwaalboom was watching a white woman leaving a general store with groceries and a black woman in her employment who was quite old carrying them, the vehicle she drove was a 'backie' a different name to a 'ute' vehicle as they are described in Australia, they are open at the back with a bench type seat in the front. As the white woman got in to drive away, she did so without checking or even caring it seemed whether the old lady had gotten into the rear open element, as she drove off the old lady was still mounting herself into the back of this truck, to my astonishment as she had just put her first leg over the side panel, her standing leg was still on the ground, she had to make a really strenuous act to lever herself and the shopping into the open deck of the rear of the backie. To the white woman it seemed it was not her problem if she got in or not, or even how, as she had already got into the vehicle and that was all that mattered.

If the old lady had not got in and had fallen off the vehicle onto the road, this would have been oblivious to the driver as it seemed to me, she didn't really care whether she was able to get in in or not, a most disturbing sight of superiority on the part of the driver.

In the early days stopping at junctions always as a passenger being a student and all that. I observed the road signage would generally have bullet holes in them, when I asked what is this all about, I was told, some white people out of boredom, and even at 'robots' (traffic lights) would shoot them up for gun practice. Practice for what I am not sure.

Where I was accommodated had few amenities, being a games room which had a tv and a table tennis.

Over those six months I got to be quite good at table tennis. Eventually beating everyone except a guy called Iain, who insisted on his given name being spelt properly on the chalk board!

In the early nights staying on site in this compound very rarely looking at South African TV which was mostly in Afrikaans and would show from time to time Dallas, that night would be a special night! Also Wimbledon would be shown.

I remember watching on tv Jimmy Connors beating Ivan Lendl, with aplomb, it was such a good game to watch it absorbed me for several hours and somehow transported me from the place I was staying, but always wished he could do the same to Borg, but somehow he had the hex on him at Wimbledon and never could, yet could beat him anywhere else, allowing him to gain titles there each year, but I digress!

I befriended a resident site engineer on the adjacent site constructing a different element of this large cement factory being built. He was much better accommodated than myself as he was senior staff and had very nice living quarters of a newly built complex used to house such site personnel with this accommodation going on to be part of the new town expansion to house all the workers at this cement factory.

He had what was known as a 'mama' which was basically a house servant where he would simply throw his clothes off at night and the following day, these items would be washed and neatly folded in his wardrobe. Now these 'mamas' came from far and wide and obviously had a need to phone their friends and family whom in general lives vast kilometres away in various provinces. This had led to large phone bills to the household, but this 'problem' was overcome by simply having a phone that was fitted with a lock, so it was not usable. These mamas got wise to this, and it was not unknown for them to carry amongst their belongings a phone on which to simply plug it in to the phone line and continue this practice of phoning their loved ones and friends far and wide!

I had been told along the way never to do your own washing and put on the line overnight as, as sure as eggs was eggs, in the morning all items of clothing would be gone, this was not a problem for me as we had laundry services but it did happen (only once)! To one of the site engineers who also lived in private quarters supplied by the company away from the site huts of the plebs, whom duly informed us of such a theft. It seemed to me the place was full of night crawlers.

The canteen within the huts served only the basic of basic foods and give us carry outs. Although some engineers with cars could drive to goodness knows where to buy stuff at lunchtime, but I never had seen any shops outside the one or two in Dwaalboom, perhaps I presume that is where they went.

At night times sometimes you would get thirsty, the water was an external tap, you could go to the kitchen as I once did and asked for milk, this came in the form of powder form, it was duly infilled with water, I was unaware it had to be drunk there and then, as before I got back to my site hut, with the dry heat and all that, it had solidified in my cup and was therefore undrinkable.

Sometimes for a '*jol*' it was possible at night to leave the camp as some of the guys did in their 'utes' which were very common in South Africa, this fun activity was simply a spin to the 'lone tree' as that was probably the most interesting part of the town which I can only describe as something out of the wild west. It wasn't exactly fun, but something to do.

Another thing about Dwaalboom and working there, the was a complete lack of women working on the construction site, but at the time I think that was a global thing, it certainly helped out on accommodation issues which I have said were basic.

One man on site lived very close to Dwaalboom, in accommodation supplied by the company, and I visited him one night I knew it had extra bedrooms, he never answered the door for a long time but when he did, he was surprised, he was an 'escaped' Rhodesian, whom had one eye, he was constantly drunk, but not in the sense of staggering around but in his general countenance and breath. After visiting his patch (forgive the pun he had one eye), the huts weren't so bad as he was completely bonkers, furthermore he came across as perverse. He was known on site as *Arthur Bonkers* (as his surname rhymed with this last word) and he certainly was.

Of the houses in the town of which there were few, before the construction of a new building complex for the workers required for the new cement factory which would make it a much bigger town, it would probably be better described as a village, with these new buildings built of high quality. I don't recall such buildings being constructed to afford any other race groups except whites, but this is only my recollection but probably true.

I recall the shopkeepers being Afrikaans with very little English, so rather than attempt in such a short time this Dutch dialect, one would buy items by pointing and using the number of digits required, money as in all cases was easy to count.

I often wondered why anyone would live in Dwaalboom, the most outermost of outskirts of civilisation, with no amenities at all and I guessed this type of living, was for the hardy or poorest alone. The positive aspects of course were the temperate weather, the solitude, it would remain to be seen what affect a population explosion would have on this tiny community, although it struck me that there were no signs of protest from the locals.

Over the months the visiting of Dwaalboom for an evening's entertainment diminished from one visit to none. It is almost impossible to write about Dwaalboom as it had so little of anything of note, perhaps that was its 'beauty'...

I actually think living in the huts mundane that it was, fostered in me the sense of ex pat lifestyle as you found that people going to a strange or foreign land that they tend to stick together, but this ex pat lifestyle was very hit and miss as the Italians that formed a large swath of immigrants or maybe they were Portuguese, I couldn't tell as they tended to stick with one and other, so did the rock spiders and us brits made up this mottley crew, but sadly Apartheid started to seep into us all by varying degrees that a sense of superiority was garnered in these separated forms of accommodation and acted to reinforce the status quo albeit, unbeknown to us it was crumbling fast due to external pressures placed upon this country.

If I'm being honest, I don't think at the time anybody within the bubble I was in, could see the regime coming to an end, as by only being there for only five minutes, how could you tell. As a country it seemed to be extremely well run, severely strict for sure, with not a great deal of crime. I could not imagine the powers that be wanting to lose power, as this could as mentioned have a dangerous effect on the whites, and also the economy.

The only signs of unrest I could see, or should I say the aftermath, was the black workers coming back from their home lands, sporting various injuries after a long weekend, but of course being a segregated system meant you could only see or perhaps want to see things. You would never enquire about such things as you wouldn't talk to candidly or socially to people not from the same race group.

A last note on Dwaalboom is I will never see it again; I made zero impression on it as could be said of anyone in most walks of life and I certainly won't be visiting it again.

Chapter 5

Accommodation

The cement factory construction project was a large one, so this meant to accommodate the construction personnel required temporary accommodation.

Some of the more senior site staff were given rented accommodation in and around the site, but this was limited solely to the senior staff. The remaining construction workers were accommodated in temporary accommodation in the three camps, the white hut, the coloured hut and the black hut. The actual standards of the huts in terms of kitchen and toilette affairs, I have suspicions where not to the same standard for each hut, but that is only a suspicion.

Each of these huts comprised numerous lines of single bed units of about twenty, which at the end of these rows would contain showers and wc's. There was a kitchen mess area to eat one's meals.

The showers didn't have a supply of hot water, but in reality, there was no need, as when the 'cold' water flowed from the showers it was always warm due obviously to the ambient temperatures which had the effect of making you long for an actual cold shower.

Meals in the morning and evening were at set times, but the kitchen would remain open for water and the like but not extra food. This was essentially what the white huts comprised. In essence utilitarian metal panelled units without heating facilities or air conditioning but acceptable non the less.

The coloured hut I am led to believe was constructed upon similar lines but their appeared to be fewer coloured people than white people, and judging by the numbers it seemed to me the sleeping rooms were not single, but its not something I can say with any authority.

The black hut however, I visited just the once (Chapter 9). However, when passing it on occasion I would notice the workers not using shower facilities, but rather hoses, hosing themselves down after a day's work which would suggest that there were no shower rooms.

The black hut as mentioned was not provided with a shuttle service to transport the workers to and from site, one could argue simply because of the vast number of workers but it was more likely that this service was not available to them, this site however was situated a little closer to site than both the white and coloured huts and I suppose just as well, but sitting in a shuttle bus, thinking to myself, I wouldn't want to walk this distance to and from the black hut to site as it was too long a trek. As for the provision of free food as was the preserve of the white hut, I would doubt, due to the sheer number of workers, the same for sleeping arrangements, it would be an uninformed guess that sleeping quarters were shared.

I do remember the black hut as being sited on a huge tract of land, which had on it a 'playing' field for playing football. The ground itself was well suited to a football field as the site and its surroundings were marked with their decidedly flatness of terrain.

The good thing about the shuttle bus was that after its rounds, you still had a chance of going to site if you missed it as it would return to the white hut upon completing its rounds, but being late didn't hardly happen but on occasion it did happen. There was no incentive at all to throw a sickie as sitting in a cabin all day was akin to sitting in a prison cell which I often likened them to.

Work in itself is like work is everywhere, it's a means to an end, but that part of the day on reflection was the best part of the day as at least one's mind was occupied to some extent.

After work the canteen was full and noisy with each ethnic group sitting with each other as typically ex pats do, it was always a noisy affair with our Italian friends needing to be as loud as possible!

After the mess period was over, some would shower, after that, each respective group would meet up in the games room or tv room, which were sparsely populated, certainly the tv mostly in Afrikaans and news based programmes that held little interest to me and it would seem anyone.

Darts was popular and the odd rock spider would participate in this activity, but always with a bottle of something for comfort. Us students on very rare occasions would be in the possession of a 'tray' of *Lion* or *Castle* lager, the local brews, but not very often.

The table tennis tables were our refuge, I remember one lad, an English speaking south African whom didn't mind mixing with the lower class immigrant white to play table tennis with us. I remember he was extremely good at table tennis, I myself wasn't very good, but trust me doing this night upon night their does come a point where you can be as good as the best player, as for the best player, his standard has no real scope of improving, but paradoxically it does improve as once the remaining players get to that standard, they find a way of developing new strategies based on their opponents improved skill levels to develop better skills. I do remember during the course of this time beating him once, to which he asked to play a further game, to which I refused as I didn't want my moment to be quashed before it had begun. In the next game and thereafter, he simply upped his game and beat me every single time.

My standard was such that to beat me was also an achievement, and I remember one Scottish guy a site agent, playing me numerous of times after reaching the same standard for the aforementioned reasons, playing me game after game for an evening and almost beat me save a stroke of luck I had on game point when a return of mine clipped the edge of the table so he couldn't react to return the ball in time and thus lost. He was most annoyed whilst I was quite smug about it. But after about three or four months of table tennis we collectively got bored and stopped playing altogether. So, we managed to occupy ourselves by playing cards instead.

In the early days of staying in the white hut, as one does, I took up jogging in the evening. I did this for two evenings in a row, the second time jogging in the middle of nowhere on a road going to nowhere as far as I was concerned, I was met by a baboon, who bounded towards me and stopped about 5m away from me and the road, every now and then, it would scamper parallel to the road to observe me once more. I remember feeling terrified of this animal and some of the same species behind it, but all I could do was continue my jog and hope not to be attacked, which I duly wasn't and once returning to the hut decided to retire from jogging with immediate effect and to my credit I have not till this day broken this pledge which could be a measure of my fortitude if it wasn't born out of cowardice!

I had mentioned that the white hut accommodated one person per cabin, but that is not entirely true, because as we were classified as students and not workers per se. I was afforded a room comprising two beds, one occupied by a fellow student and it is without doubt as true a saying as any that familiarity breeds contempt. However, with my young ego I thought it was him who was the most dreadful person one had the misfortune to spend a room with each night, but the feeling was mutual.

After many months it came to a head our resentment to one another. It was a most grim experience working and living like this, comforted only really by the weather and at some point thinking Grimsby didn't seem so bad after all.

In fairness, the accommodation, the white hut provided clean bed clothes every day and the wc and shower units were always spotless, but creature comforts of those, where few. In those days, letter writing was the thing and if appropriate some of our work colleagues would share reading out their messages from home, which as sad as it is writing this, was such a comfort to hear of other people's stories. When receiving a letter of any kind lifted the mood of the evening and following day, with re reading of such letters a thing to do to try and relive the thrill of getting a letter, prompting one and all into letter writing.

In those six months spent in the Northern Transvaal I do not recall a single rainfall event, which is why I suppose the huts never came with rain water goods. The huts themselves being of metal had no sound insulation and it was easy to hear one's neighbour's conversations, as it happens, my 'cell' was C10 and at the end of a row, so I could only eaves drop on one side, but this was pointless as the language I heard was foreign and not often as it was single occupied, but when conversations did happen it became a source of irritation.

I remember thinking what it must be like to be in prison, as to me this was prison as we had a specific date for the return flights which meant the stay in the hut was indeed a sentence as such, it was strange how that made you feel, knowing you just couldn't go home if you had had enough, I know I had, but must bear it, it would have been easy of course if the times being had were enjoyable.

Nearer the end of my stay, rooming with my roommate as noted fraught with resentment and tension, it came as a great surprise that he came up to me to tell me he had been transferred to another site. I truly was glad for him, but these feelings of freedom from him were quickly dispelled as he was replaced by another student to C10, this guy I forget his name, was if it could be possible, even more boring than my previous roommate to the point I started missing 'the good old day's'!

In all that time we had a single party in C10 which comprised either slab of *Castle* or *Lion* beer (does it matter!?) With the party abruptly coming to an end once all the cans had gone, which was about two cans each, my new roommate was disgusted by this behaviour and let his feelings be known by going to bed, which was pretty melodramatic when you consider going to bed meant simply getting into bed in the same room in which the party is taking place, but it had the desired affect and everyone left, that being the three or four people, or was it because the booze ran out. It seemed to me that Britain gets a bad press about being a nation of boozers, but my experience in South Africa was that drinking was a way of life, not however going to pubs, not drinking beer as such, but beer being used as a thirst quencher, the most common drink of choice was a bottle of spirits per night.

Chapter 6

Work

Work, now that's a phrase for a student sent to a foreign land, whose main objective is to have fun, not work! Notwithstanding upon arrival on site, I was introduced to the site personnel, the site engineers, surveyors, site managers, quality control and of course the site agent. After a brief conversation and issue of personnel protection equipment, I was allocated a desk in the site engineer's cabin.

Thereafter for a number of weeks my sole job was to stand in a particular area of the site where the workers were constructing excavations into which would be poured reinforced concrete foundations, this wasn't in fact work at all and fairly quickly I got bored of this and began exploring the adjoining site and befriended the resident engineer there, whom for some reason I got on with famously. Site staff including myself had walkie talkie to facilitate communication, but it was quickly used by times as a means of finding out where I was.

As the work basically for most part, was standing by observing the general operatives and ensuring they worked efficiently, this was a difficult task in the sense it was so boring, difficult not in the way physical work is of course, so this wandering off became my norm to visit this resident engineer, whom was involved in a number of large circular silos being constructed, this being part of the same project done by another contractor, required concrete bored piles which for added strength had to be reamed at the bottom to widen out the bearing area and hence increase the bearing capacity of the pile. The piles were constructed in a very stiff clay ideal to provide friction grip and end bearing strength, it also however meant the resident engineer had to be lowered down these bored piles which were constructed using an auger to drill through the ground. This man was lowered down in a bucket from a winched cable, armed with a torch and measuring tape. One day he asked me to join him, which I promptly did, we were winched some 18m below ground in the bored hole unprotected from collapse, (nowadays this would be done by a fibre optic).

Once down there, Richard would measure the diameter of the widened out base and its pitch back to the main 1.4m diameter of the pile to ensure the under-reaming was done in a satisfactory manner, which it always was, as the black workers in general took great pride in their work, but would easily be sacked otherwise, no such thing as trade unions there. For me it was a marvel to go into an open excavated circular hole unprotected from collapse, this was made possible due to the stiffness of this sub-strata.

Eventually I was given a job in quality control to stop these wanderings, which involved using a theodolite to measure the plumb of the newly formed column shutters, to check for accuracy in both orthogonal directions, this check was done when the formwork charge hand, a Cape of Good Hope coloured man, called Victor would go by the quality control cabin to notify me, to allow myself time to mobilise my theodolite to check the plumbness of the formwork prior to pouring concrete. Unbeknown to us both one of the site excavator operatives took a photograph of both myself and Victor without our knowledge, it was a great photograph as it was done with neither of us aware of being photographed and captured a real moment in time.

This photograph I have had on my desk for years and as with most things it eventually was lost.

Victor died on site a very short time after I had got to know him. (R.I.P). As one day a worker was asked to move the tower cranes slings to ground from their position, two storeys above ground level. These slings were made of metal chains and very heavy, so rather than take them down in a singular manner via the stairwell, he decided to push them off the side of the second floor, just as Victor was walking underneath this (raw mill) building, as did most people accessing and egressing the site. Now as the chains fell to the ground somebody shouted to Victor 'look out'!!! In a booming voice, all this did was make Victor instinctively look up, it mattered not as no safety helmet would have saved him anyway, as the slings smashed into his face and killed him instantly.

There was no lamentation, no enquiry from a safety body and in fact only an ambulance to take his remains away, with site construction continuing unabated.

As it happened the other Cape Coloured's who were mostly charge hands were given some days off to attend his funeral many kilometres away in Cape Town.

This made me realise how dangerous a site could be, to my knowledge I am almost certain the worker that threw the crane slings was sacked and sent home but not charged with anything as no police were called.

Perhaps on a lighter note after such a tragedy, some months later I was caught coming into work late by the contracts manager who would fly up to site in the company's two seater jet plane as one does, every two weeks to see how the works were progressing. I knew of his arrival and went to the shuttle bus in which the driver was obliged to drive me to site. I stopped short of the site and went towards my site office by an unscripted route, but this guy was standing there after a head count. He was a rock spider called Shirt de Bxxx (only rock spiders seemed to have these Dutch type surnames), he espied my arrival and promptly walked up to me and asked me why I was late? To his amazement I said I slept in because I had stayed up watching Dallas!

I wonder has anyone in the world ever been saved from the sack by using this excuse?! He said, 'so what'! that was all he said as it threw him completely as to how this could actually be an excuse and it rendered him speechless thereafter, so I simply left him there pondering and returned to my site office desk, fully expecting him to follow me but he never did.

I remember once being given a task to provide excavation levels for the formation of a large foundation, which meant standing by the sight level. It used to be called a dumpy level, which were difficult to attain a horizontal sighting, but they became obsolete with the onset of the automatic level which as the word says balanced itself automatically. This task was an all day affair, which meant standing by the dig and giving levels every now and then with a site measuring staff to ensure the dig was not too shallow or wasn't excavated too deep. During this period, one of the white South African foremen, came up to me and asked to use it at another location, I told him no, but he was Afrikaans and simply took it from where I was working with it, with complete distain as in this world Afrikaner's were number one to any other members of the so called white race group, so he only asked in curtesy, but in fact displayed none.

Whilst there, a London student from another university arrived a week or so after myself, he considered himself above myself the only other student, because he was reading at a university whilst I was doing so at a Polytechnic. In passing that is why there are no polytechnics now as such graduates couldn't obtain work as easily as university students due to a perceived snobbery that university students were superior even though the examining board was one and the same. He 'assisted' me in my quality control checks. I always remember the day he left a few weeks before I was to restart my semester in my college, by these farewell words, 'You have all been average..' knowing, he was able to ventilate his feelings towards his fellow workers as he was now in a position of strength now that he was about to leave by taxi and able therefore to let people know what he thought of them, this angered me, as I had looked after him in the first few weeks until he got his confidence, but hey ho.

On occasion if the site agent decreed after say some construction target had been hit or if it was somebody with white skins birthday, a *fleis Braai* (meat cooked) aka a BBQ was had on site after work hours for people to stand around for a 'jol' and a get together. Conversations generally arose about the terrible Americans and their sanction's, and I remember one man saying in earnest 'at least we didn't kill anyone to get our land', to this statement, I would find hard to believe when thinking about all the cape coloured as they were known being the offspring of the early settlers. Other conversations went along the lines of 'well we built it so it's ours, and the old chestnut, 'if it wasn't for the white man'... and so on. If you wanted to talk sport, then merely mention Rugby and all you had to do then was sit back and listen to how fabulous South Africa was at it, to be fair to them, they were indeed. There rugby league is the Currie Cup and it's a complete talking point to them if you know anything about that sport, but for me it was a no thankyou! It seemed to me like it was their religion as opposed to being a sport.

Back to the *braai*. The black workers would stand around after work hours, rather like vultures to eat up the leftovers when us whites had finished and had left, it was a most ugly sight, looking at grown men to be that hungry, (desperate days for some).

Back to sadness again, one of these men got up one morning very early before work started, dressed in his best attire and went up one of the newly constructed buildings and promptly jumped off to his death. On that occasion although an ambulance came, nobody was allowed off site to go to his funeral, as somehow through blind ignorance from myself and collectively all the site staff, nobody cared and again work carried on just the same without any such thing as an enquiry from any authority, again if there was such a thing. Life was indeed cheap in South Africa.

Sometimes when it was a white man's birthday, they would get a slab of beer to celebrate, by sending the shuttle bus to down town Dwaalboom to get it, so for an hour or so in the middle of the working day we would all get a beer or two, quite how that conforms to health and safety was not a consideration and you would generally wander around the site thereafter and try and not fall down an open excavation because as you have guessed, open excavations where never protected by safety barriers.

I was tasked one day and delighted to do so, to drive a 'backie' to a place some 100km away to pick up some piece of plant, but with a worker to physically place it in the vehicle. The drive was on dirt track roads with me stopping on occasion to ask people (only white people), for further directions. I had seen this before where the black worker would be made to ride in the back of the open deck vehicle despite there being at least two further seats in the cabin. I was not to be one of those people. Instead, after he lighted onto the back of the vehicle, I summonsed him in to sit with me for the several hours drive, it was after a very short time the cabin was overcome with intense body odour from this man, I stopped the backie and simply pointed to the back for him to ride in the open deck.

This man like many other had no real facilities for personal hygiene and it was quite impossible to sit in a boiling hot cab with such an unfortunate person, still, for what it's worth, he too was delighted to be on the drive, away from the daily routine of site life. I still feel bad about this so many years later but do not think I would be able to do things any different, as the poor man stank to high heaven through no fault of his own.

Site communication was done with a two-way radio back to head office which was available to us once a week for families able to radio their loved ones from the company's head offices from various offices in principle cities, but mostly from Joburg, but for me there was no need. But all ex pats were allowed hang around and listen in, simply because any communication was better than any communication and the radio room would generally be full to the rafters.

One day one poor man in front of his listening colleagues received a message from his wife to inform him she had left him; we didn't speak to him for several days thereafter as he had a countenance of a zombie the poor man.

One other form of communication of course was the letter as mentioned already but touched on again here. It was an amazing exciting feeling to get a letter from home or a loved one if you had one, it put you in mind how vital this service must have been to the men of war in both world wars as there was a distinct boon in one's demeanour upon receipt of a letter that sustained you for several days.

There was even a telephone, which could be booked to make a call home, with the cost taken out of your wages, I used this service only once as it was quite expensive those days.

Whilst there, I began to like the lifestyle on offer for someone like me. I never thought of the morals of such thinking, but merely of the chance to work in warmer climes after my graduation.

I thence went and had an interview with Richard's consultancy practice. At the interview I didn't come across very well or indeed clever, one of the questions was 'what is Bernoulli's theorem? To this question I couldn't answer, but know it ever more as follows: Energy in a pipe comprises pressure head, velocity head and potential head, but knowing this some weeks later never held me in good stead and no job offer or sponsorship was offered.

Another task of mine was to check the reinforcement as placed against the reinforced steel schedule drawing done, prior to concrete pours to ensure all the reinforcement was placed as substantially accurately as possible in accordance with the construction drawings, this task was responsible enough but not physical in nature.

I was in awe of these workers using the 20kg to 60kg metal reusable metal formwork panels pinned together with lugs in the baking sun and placed to form the various building elements in reinforced concrete.

This work was labour intensive in the extreme and in reality, not needed, as the plywood formwork alternative was available but used very rarely for places where metal shutters couldn't be used due to pipework cut outs and the like. These metal shutters were super-efficient in terms of re-use but the trade-off was how labour intensive as it was, but this was not considered an issue to the construction companies in general at that time.

Another cost saving measure was all concrete was mixed on site from large cylindrical concrete batch silos, which allowed the basic constituents of concrete; sand, aggregate and cement, to be mixed in various proportions to achieve the different grades of concrete. I would notice from time to time the concrete would go '*cold*', that is a 'cold joint' would appear in the concrete pour as the placed concrete would set before the pour was finished, this was due to many reasons, mostly the size of pours would generally be ambitious and also the logistics of placing concrete in such hot weather relying on concrete made from a single batch source. In almost all cases the 'cold joint' wouldn't affect the structural integrity of the built element.

In construction, there are always construction joints, placed so as not to affect the structural integrity. But such cold joints were always jack hammered down as labour and materials were generally cheap and it gave the client represented by the resident engineer the authority to impose such instructions to demolish and rebuilt, sometimes I felt it was just because they could, but work was cheap labour and could be done anyway for the sake of it.

Back to Arthur *Bonkers*, Arthur had a strange appearance with his glass eye, he hailed from the Netherlands and I was his assistant in the quality control section. He was strange in the sense, that he was desperate to fit in and I was told would speak in Afrikaans in this desperation to be regarded as an Afrikaner. Although behind his back he was a figure of fun and because of his eye problems couldn't do his job very well which gave me therefore a role on this site.

When the workers were given orders, they would invariably be given orders in Afrikaans, quite how they understood this language was beyond me, particularly the men from Botswana.

Site washing and toilet facilities whereas with most things separate along the lines of race with always a worker commandeered to keep these facilities clean.

The white toilets were spotless and per capita quite acceptable as was the coloureds toilets, but alas the black toilets were decidedly inadequate in both numbers and hygiene but this issue, if it was an *issue* at all, was largely overlooked.

As mentioned earlier I would visit my friend from the other site still, on a daily basis, as my tasks didn't fill an hour let alone a shift, so my walkie talkie was still being used to see where I was. I would generally know when a column needed checking, but on occasion get it wrong and get these messages to come back to site.

I did get reprimanded on occasion about this, but this largely fell on deaf ears as to my mind it didn't affect construction progress and besides I'm sure they didn't want to pay for a new plane flight, as even though this wasn't ideal to my temporary employees. I also didn't like working on a building site especially in South Africa with its inherent dangers ignored largely and the work I did do was productive nonetheless.

I remember that in the southern hemisphere surveying uses southern (positive) and western (positive) co-ordinate system, whereas in the UK surveying uses northern (positive) and easting (positive) setting out systems. Our site had a setting out point from which our surveyor set out the various elements of the cement factory but erroneously used eastings and northings, but as the setting out point was on the site as a start point the setting out although set out in the wrong quadrant mattered little as the land was so vast and the set out in the grand scheme of things did not become an issue, merely requiring re-alignment of the railway lines that were to service this site and was considered not a major catastrophe as the land was so vast, this *faux pas* happened because the surveyor was Scottish and was not aware that he was to use southern and westings, and kept his job!

Chapter 7

Long weekends

Working on site was a six-day affair and working and living in such a remote place was no bad thing, as it meant Sunday was the only downtime that had to be endured. Some of the more established site staff were given living quarters as regaled previously as well as company cars and accommodation away from the huts, their living quarters where in what can only be described as a cluster of houses in the one place, the redeeming factor for them was that there was a tennis court, but as only one other person could play a little beside myself, it was a rare respite from the boredom, also it was rare for us graduates to be invited to the engineers quarters as some snobbery existed, but out of desperation, some of us guys would inveigle ourselves to be invited away from the hut!

But once a month this status quo of wanting a game of tennis on our down day Sunday changed at the occurrence of the Long Weekend. It was like it was a holiday the mood it created collectively, the two days off for the weekend of the Saturday and Sunday, wow!

These weekends meant driving to the nearest town, that being Johannesburg. But Joburg was such a long drive of circa twelve hours and therefore we all needed to assist in driving one of the site engineers' cars, to ensure we would have some time to party meant we travelled non stop. Our party comprised two graduates and three site engineers to Joburg, the way we accomplished this was, when designated driver A would drive whilst everyone slept and only when he would temporarily nod off, the car would invariably jolt, to awaken us passengers, signalling the change of driver, this phenomenon would occur throughout the journey until we hit the fabled land that was Joburg. Quite were we stayed depended on whether we were lucky or not! Which meant the car anywhere but the car!

Our place of choice was Hillbrow, as it was a district suitably rough and ready for the likes of ourselves and had lots of bars and nightclubs. Our favourite of these places was a club called '*Boobs*'! this name for the club really tickled me and the irony was I never did get any!

For some reason this was always the place we would descend on at the latter parts of the night before closing time at 2am which was strictly adhered to by all the licenced premises. (The underground premises were never re-visited again by my group).

Notwithstanding after several libations of alcohol girls didn't seem to matter, I read once in more recent years, in a survey done on the best time to meet a woman on a night out, was 7pm (who does these surveys)?! With the reasoning men at that time of night are still relatively able to communicate with the opposite sex, because after that, forget it, the booze would win almost always, certainly in South Africa where young white women, whether they were pretty or not, their stock was about ten times higher than it was in the UK, and the threshold level of the would be suiter would be most definitely lower!

In *Boobs* one night I remember having a fairly enjoyable conversation with a female civil servant girl, trying to chat her up and her declaring 'oh so you're an immigrant', this took me aback! as I had never been labelled in such a manner, it was a light switch moment, as only then did I understand to a degree what racism is, it as I remember well, gave me a feeling of inferiority which in many ways is also the human condition. I did meet one beautiful girl and getting along famously me thought, but alas I was not of her class! In every sense including my 3rd class in this system.

On another occasion I slept or tried to sleep in a stairwell as it offered some shelter, but I guess in those days, the powers of recovery were good from no sleep or stupendous hangovers, my, did we drink those weekends after escaping from site for more than a day, drank like no tomorrow but luckily tomorrow always came.

One of the lads had a penchant for chatting up girls in front of their boyfriends, one reason being he didn't mind having a scrap, but the main reason really was white women were as rare as the proverbial rocking horse …

In all the times we went on our long weekends I do not recall ever seeing a beggar, I don't know why that is, but think it could because of the grinding poverty that existed amongst the black people there, there was not exactly any charity to give round. I might be wrong on that. It brings me back to Britain that observation, as where I live now, most of the beggars are professional beggars, though nowhere to be seen when it rains! They are generally chirpy and polite (the professional ones) and make a pretty penny too with this trick, leaving the real destitute devoid of confidence and hope in the background in truly dire straits, I have no truck for these professional beggars.

On a lighter side back in Hilbrow, one of the settled ex pats was moving from one apartment to the other. He being a scouser and the message was lost in translation when he was at work one day whilst the removal people were moving his stuff. Part of his belongings included a budgerigar, and somehow, not explained by the removal company it had died during this event. So, my work colleague, received a message one day on site, from the removal company via the two way radio to the site, he was not there to field the call, but the message passed onto him was something like this 'your bird is dead', when he got this message and as he was a scouser, in scouse language meant his girlfriend! He was beside himself and we all tried to console him, he was given permission by the site agent to use his phone to make arrangements and phoned his girlfriend's place of work in Joburg only to hear his girlfriend talk back to him, and then have to console her for the loss of the budgie! He did get a bit of stick of us after that though.

One of these such weekends rather than admit defeat and return to the car, me and a pal went searching for accommodation, hotels were off limits, so we approached a housing tower block and the janitor guy who must of known his tenants where not home, heard our tale, then took money off us and brought us to a habituated apartment were we dossed down, he told us he would be back at 6am (so not much time), sure enough he burst in on the dot and ensured we were gone within five minutes, no raiding the fridge or ablutions were to be had, but better than the car or just walking around.

As it happened it would be no bad thing to amble the streets all night as within this strict regime police officers were armed, and it was safe to do so and indeed the weather was such you would not freeze, however drinking all night was not an option because they had surprisingly strict licencing hours.

Nearer the end of my stay, I befriended a Scottish Engineer in the white hut, whose family emigrated to South Africa and lived in Joburg, after that my accommodation issues on long weekends was pas de problème. One night he met a girl and promptly went back to his place (his parents), to do what one does, but being inventive enough I went back to his place, a high rise block, I managed to avoid the concierge and 'broke in' via a pre-arranged open window. I stupidly went sneaking to his room with the idea of sleep, but when switching on his light I saw both he and her fast asleep naked on top of the bed.

I was awakened in the living room by a golden coloured dog licking my face followed by the Scot's guys mother, she asked me why oh why had I not slept in Donny's room? I couldn't tell her save saying I prefer to sleep on my own, some more hours passed in the morning and Donny managed to get rid of his conquest without his mother knowing, he would bitterly complain, that it was all right living at *haim*, but it was always difficult getting rid of a girl without his mother finding out, butter wouldn't melt, his mother adored him.

That afternoon I stayed in this flat and with his parents and remember it being a very pleasant thing to be in a loving family atmosphere and to have creature comforts.

On another occasion with him and his Scottish ex pat friends we drank so much I passed out in a park, and they just carried on and on until I awoke and joined in again. Donny was incredibly homesick for Scotland, and I owned a pair of *Umbro* football short, he simply had to have as in those day's sports apparel shops didn't exist and these things were as close to wearing leisure clothes with a distinct ex pat theme to them, he never took them off, on site, everywhere until they simply wore out. It must be said if not for Donny, with such an effervescent personality, I would have been stuck, as I was never really made friends with the other guys, we students were a means to an end type friend to be used only for long weekends by being part time drivers to assist in the journey for the site engineers, in fact I recall one long weekend being marooned in the white hut, *Billy no mates*, mark two!

Hillbrow was a mixture of music, pubs, secret drinking dens and anything goes, one Sunday Donny brought me to a secret drinking den and it was such an eye opener to me, how so many people circumnavigated the licencing laws.

He was part of the scene in Hillbrow and some English speaking South African guy wanted to be English, he pointed out this guy in *Boobs* who had created for himself a fake English accent he developed and when asked where was he from, he would always say 'Plymouth' without realising this misguided adopted place of origin was not pronounced as he did. This was a standing joke for those around when asking him where he was from. As he would say 'ply' as in a layer of wood instead of 'pli' as in plimsoles.

Hillbrow a suburb in Joburg was a place that had a character all of its own, I could only compare it with being akin with Soho in London. It felt seedy, (it was seedy!), but us young guys liked to go there on these long weekends, no sightseeing for us. I think the reason Hillbrow was our choice of destination was because one of the site engineers had been going there before I arrived and so it continued, the other districts in this city I didn't get to know the names of any, but do recall being with one of the engineers trying to buy a flat in a district called Ladysmith but that was some kilometres outside of Joburg, so Joburg it was, it was a great escape from the mundane that was living and working on site six days a week.

In some instances, as with all places, what went on in Hillbrow, stayed in Hillbrow, save to say at the time it was my most favourite place on earth. I even met another engineer who actually worked in Joburg, he told me that on Fridays, they would go to their office roof for a few cold ones before going home for the weekend. I really did at the time think this was the life and I had set my heart on going back there to live after graduation until life got in the way, as it always does and much quicker than I had fully appreciated what a bad system it was, which I can only put down to being immature.

I don't know how we did it, but we would spend all the daylight time in Joburg before setting back to our place of work, this to maintain the sense of freedom for as long as possible before the hum drum that was Dwaalboom.

One of the ex pats we got to know one weekend whose name will be kept secret but known as Charlie, met, and got off with, a black woman which was a complete no no. I am not sure how he met her with all meeting places segregated, so I must presume it was in an underground club. He told us he went back to her place in Soweto, the well-known township outside of Joburg, and to his amazement her parents got out of their bed to allow Ricky and his new girlfriend a place to sleep, as I'm sure they did eventually. The thing he boasted about most was that in the morning, his new girlfriends' parents cooked him some breakfast before they sent him on his merry way.

So, driving back was always a melancholy affair, with the drive being even more harum-scarum. But being young we somehow managed to get back, with driver changes, a bit more frequent.

Driving back had none of the zest of going to Joburg, but we would always get back in good time as in reality even though it was such long distances to travel, the route we took meant there was not much in the way of traffic to hold us up.

This is but a tale of a young white man's experience of a long weekend, I must confess of not getting to know any other people not of this so called group, so never knew what they did at these times.

I was aware however that the black workers would be bussed from site at the start of the long weekends, I guess to a train station and make their ways to their local tribes, the main destination was Botswana as most of the site workers lived there, with most coming from a place called Gaborone the capital.

One of the students from the previous year had been to South Africa for his work experience placement, let's just call him Dave (because that was his name), he told us that he went to Swaziland which was an internal part of South Africa that was not recognised internationally, it was a homeland for the African's. Here, anything goes as previously narrated, he told us, he was there one weekend because there was a pre season tournament which featured Spurs and Liverpool.

He told us he and his pals in the evening, slipped through security to the players only lounge for a drinks evening, because as they were young white men, the security didn't recognise them as being not one of these clubs players, so they spend the evening in the company of both Liverpool and Spurs as *faux* players!

He said he had got off with two black ladies together, he said he didn't have to pay them and had an eventful evening and morning with them.

When coming back home, he said he was greeted by his wife, the only person of his party to be met at the station, who ran to him to welcome him oblivious of his indiscretions.

Back to the long weekends: One Monday I espied one of the black workers, who returned to site with an opened up nose with part his nose cartilage missing, this exposed area was very pink where part of his nose once was. His and many other black people went back to their homelands for these weekends and got involved in fights with rival tribes, with the weapon of choice most definitely the machete, but not confined to this weapon, as any weapon will do.

From reflecting on the details of the two site deaths and seeing such wounds first hand as stated already. Life was to my way of thinking was valued in a lesser way than I felt it should. I was told of police brutality to deal with civil unrest when it occurred which it did, but never did I see anything of that kind, being as we were, far removed as possible by working in Dwaalboom, this place on that basis was no bad a place to live.

Several months after returning to the UK, one of my drive buddies with whom I'd shared trips to Joburg with, had fell asleep whilst driving back to Dwaalboom, however he and his party never got back that early morning but instead crashed into a slow moving goods train at a level crossing and while all his mates were OK, he remained in hospital for several months wearing some form of head plastercast. I met him again several years later, quite by chance in London and quickly became one of the members of the Friday club in the West End but that's another story.

Chapter 8

Boredom

When looking back on things, especially such a thing as Apartheid, the recollection captures all sorts of forgotten times and ways that are no longer, a lost world so to speak, no bad thing as in this instant. Even when going back to places in more recent times, those places where you have spent time are gone, gone forever and only exist in your mind if at all. So, by regaling this time, has brought me back and with a sense of melancholy because of time that has passed by so quickly. The abiding memory that has stayed with me of *that* South Africa are that of boredom (and Chapter 9)!

Boredom comes in many forms of idleness brought about by having no kith or kin, no friends or being away from home. The white hut never garnered any worthwhile friendships except for Donny. Donny for me was a life saver, he was only twenty years old and couldn't believe I was twenty two, in those burgeoning days, such an age gap was a chasm, this made me self-conscious about my age, from then on and all my life since, it seems to me Ive always been the oldest person in any party, it's amazing how powerful words are and it's important to use them wisely as negative comments to anyone can be very damaging, that is for sure.

Boredom that you get when living on your own, which is exacerbated by having no creature comforts of what you have been accustomed to. Living in the white hut, no matter how hard I try, I find it barely possible to remember anything worth remembering except that besides table tennis, cards, darts (I forgot about them), sometimes tv. That the time seemed to go at the pace of a snail on drugs. My main train of thought was counting down the days until I could depart and a promise, I made to myself never to take on a job which had a specific end term date, as somehow this leaving date manifested itself into most of my days as an obstacle I could not overcome. I had not learnt of stoicism then and lived wholly not in the now, but in the when, which is of course not living at all.

Unbeknown to me, this angst within me, was a collective one, even for the workers who lived there and could leave whenever they wanted, but constricted by finances would put paid to such fancies. However, this boredom was like being like a fish out of water conspired to dream up something that had never (I believe so) been done before, but the possibility was there due to the location of this site and the type of segregated living, these type of building sites had with their accommodation arrangements described to death hitherto!

What had this boredom done to us? Idle minds, work for the devil and all of that, but no, that was not the case, as within us all is a human spirit, a spirit of adventure lying dormant, a spirit of very many things that no one could ever imagine doing unless pushed to it. That is what boredom did to us, it pushed us to do things unrestricted by the laws of the land, to free ourselves to be what we wanted to be and do, boredom can also be a source of productivity of a positive kind if harnessed correctly.

As per mentioned, goings on were afoot to relieve this boredom, done unbeknown to myself or indeed most people, these goings on as I have called them were going on for very many months! Protocols were being tested and indeed transgressed, but done in a subversive way, but not done with any intent of a criminal nature, but laws are laws and in a very restrictive regime, very easy to fall foul of them. For instance, the police brutality at the time would mete out for the most minor of infractions, wholly inappropriate to the transgression. For black people especially or more accurately specifically, falling foul of anything resulted in a disproportionate response that are not for these pages, but must be recognised as being so, this meant that black subjugation was so intense that when the police would arrive say in Soweto or other such townships, the locals would physically run away from them. This is written and must be written in order that what follows can be understood as something that was quite remarkable in such times as they were. It is true that human nature is so strong, it has to be! This strength comes not only from within but from without, by all the people you encounter in one's journey, acting as a source of strength from encouragement or a drain as the case may be, the latter must be avoided and in this instant they most certainly were.

Without necessarily getting to the point as to what this is about, I think once the word football is mentioned, then the cat is most certainly out of the bag! With tales of suspense no longer able to be maintained. It is to that end we must reveal what was afoot, for all those long months with no one any the wiser. Quite who initiated these bi lateral talks of staging a soccer match between the black hut and the white hut I do not know.

Playing any sport along racially integrated lines was against the law, mixing in public socially was not allowed, there were black buses, and I would suppose coloured buses and to a lesser extent white buses. Trains would be compartmented. All aspects of life were as separate as it was possible to be in this jaundice country, integration was acceptable in terms of services only.

Football however is universal. It has a language of its own, it transcends every barrier that it faces simply because for almost all sports loving people, it's the peoples sport, with the exception of course being South Africa were its rugby! Whilst there, I think I recall a rebel England team touring and played the Boks three times, losing all tests, but winning some provincial matches. England was led by a Mike Smith if my memory serves me correctly, to be forever banned from international rugby thereafter.

Anyway, the unilateral, bi lateral, multi-lateral talks progressed it would seem for several months without a whiff of rumour that a football match was proposed between the black hut and the white hut. As it happened the coloured hut although had many cape coloured's, mostly had asian workers who it would seem weren't interested.

Where could such a match be played? Would it be announced by the company? Of course it couldn't be, because it was illegal and they weren't told. Playing a football match at the white hut was a no-no, as it was the preserve of whites that they could enter wherever they liked it wasn't so the other way round, and logistically it was a non-starter anyways, the white hut held about fifty or so men, whilst the black hut held as many as perhaps three hundred or even more men. Their location did have an open space and on the day of the match *did* have goal posts but no nets. It would appear that this space had been afforded to the black workers when the camp was set up, after all there was plenty of space.

The surrounding lands always had grass as did most of the country, it was usually a very pale yellow, almost tinder in appearance, except for some fields being constantly watered that made them green and lush. Also, the country wasn't as prone to drought as it is coastal, but of course in Dwaalboom in the Northern Transvaal was as parched as anywhere in Africa. That aside the proposed playing surface must have been played on so much that it was a dark grey with dust and no grass and made of iron.

When getting the shuttle bus past the black hut in the mornings and evenings I don't recall either the pitch itself or even that the hut was compounded by wire fencing. I'm not even sure if the negotiators knew what would happen, if a white team came to the black hut for such an event or what the reaction would be, but boredom ignores such small matters. The biggest hurdle would surely be the company itself allowing such an event to occur under its watch. However, it was smack bang in the middle of nowhere and never had there been a police car or the sniff of one in my time there, even after the two deaths on site.

Nevertheless, such an event could and would have had by word of mouth gained legs of it happening if disclosed in advance. So, the first I heard of the match was the mid-week immediately before the Sunday game and I was to pick the team! I think it had something to do with having the standard issue permed hair that was in vogue at the time, also youthful in appearance and perhaps could play football, the latter, was simply a pipedream, I certainly was gifted in knowing how a game was to be played but not gifted in its application!

Donny was on the team sheet first, I didn't have a team sheet per se, but he was first as at least had football shorts! Somehow, we collected a Mottley Crew of eleven players and no substitutes comprising, a Scot (Donny), two brits with the rest being mostly Italians or Portuguese, I simply don't recall, I just asked around in the evenings in the mess hall before everyone as they seemed would disappear back to their cells for the night. It wasn't strictly speaking the white hut versus the black hut; we were going to win and all the site engineers who lived off site were in the team. It never said, on the contrary, the terms of reference were not stipulated. So, on that basis these engineers could participate, and it was on that basis the spirit of the game hadn't been infringed upon as it never said nor stipulated whether they could or could not play. All that mattered was we was going to win and win by using any means possible, well I was young and impetuous!

Chapter 9

The *Happening* that couldn't happen

Immediately after this football game was arranged, the first thing to do was see who was about and who was willing to play. As it turned out quite a few wanted to play, but being such a short time to meant I could approach only those I knew and then others thereafter in the mess in the following evenings. As with all sports teams, nobody wanted to be a substitute, and as I had played that role many times myself, I made the unconscious decision we were to have eleven players only and besides there was limited space in the two shuttle buses we had and we wanted to arrive as a single unit and try and be a football team even if it was for just a day.

The following days, there was indeed a better mood throughout the building site at the prospect of doing something that we wanted to do, this excitement was enhanced not in open conversation, but in quiet conversations that didn't cross racial lines, but there was a definitive buzz about the place even though it was an open secret.

Non of us had football boots (the ground was too hard anyway), of the eleven in the team only nine of our side had training shoes. I myself had plimsoles and the goal keeper wore shoes, that was how he was selected as the goal keeper, in those days it was not a matter of simply going to a sports shop and getting kitted out as no such places existed, who would want to buy them anyway for such a one off game of football.

Sunday couldn't come quick enough, but it came non the less. The traditional Sundays in Dwaalboom, was there wasn't any, no church, no anything, so that meant we could schedule the match at the most optimum time of 2pm which was just past the hottest part of the day and plenty of time before sunset. Even this detail had not been established until we had spoken to the shuttle bus drivers who acted as informants to our hosts as to the time of our arrival. Even at this stage there was no communication between parties in an open way but on a need to know basis.

Finally it was time to go to play the game. So, we all boarded the shuttle buses, without any fanfare of well wishers, after all it wasn't as if we had any fans! We went all togged out as much as we could, the site engineers came and parked up to get on the busses also, somebody asked me did I have a football, to which I replied, 'no they have one' I presumed in my lie. I do recall the twenty minutes or so drive to the black hut and remember in a moment of paranoia that we could be set upon by going into the black hut, as there were so many people and no security, but that must be put down to nativity and apprehension of such a match being taken place in the most peculiar of circumstances.

Eventually upon arriving at the black hut, everyone in it were there to greet us at the entrance to the compound, greet us they did the place was thronging and entering the gates, we were met with cheers and smiling faces and a sense of welcome that could scarcely be believed unless you had witnessed it. They greeted us with open arms and as if we were heroes. I later put it down to the collective appreciation of the black workers being made feel equal to us, as of course they were, (perhaps not in football, but that's to come), feelings of gratitude and an acknowledgement that we perceived them in parity of esteem, all senses of superiority removed by this act of 'honouring' them with our presence, what nonsense I'm afraid, as it was really because we were bored on Sunday's too! However, it was only afterwards did I become to realise what it must feel like to be a third class citizen in your own country and then realise why they were so happy at our *grand* gesture of which we had no conception of what it must have meant to them.

Indeed, when we went to the pitch, the opposition did in fact have a ball, as well as proper goal posts which although I thought I'd seen them in passing the site, although not particularly looking, nevertheless it was nice to have proper goals, in which our shoe laden goalkeeper positioned himself. After a very short warm up which comprised, us simply looking around at each other and also all of a sudden, the realisation that it was real.

The whole of the playing surface was surrounded by the entire occupants of the black hut, making it feel like you were actually playing in a real match with the supporters jumping and shouting and waving and making a right din. It turned out the ball I had mentioned was in fact a single ball, so a warmup is not one that was done in a conventional fashion, any pre-match running routines I don't believe any of us knew how to do, or take charge to do so, so didn't. So that was our warmup simply standing looking at each other and then it was time to prepare for the game with everyone under their own volition moving to their positions of choice.

As it turned out, somehow we almost all took up different positions on the pitch, with Donny of course the centre forward (he was the centre forward because that's where he stood), I myself a midfield general (in my head), was centre mid, there was a little bit of manoeuvring of some of the players into other positions, until we eventually lined up in the 4 4 2 formation, well what would you expect? We'd never heard in those days of other systems, so it wasn't in fact a system at all, it was simply how teams line up and had done so since the year dot.

In these moments prior to kick off, we looked at our opposition, standing still in most parts, some determined, some smiling and quiet and mostly all bare foot, this last point gave me a false sense of security on how this game was going to pan out, as the ball that was produced was of the leather variety, not something that could be kicked very hard in barefoot methought.

It was *de rigueur* that there would be no referee of course, but somehow our opposition offered to allow us to kick off as after all we were white, that was the feeling I got anyway, and besides there was no referee to toss a coin or to allow the winner to elect what side to start from.

I don't even think we had agreed on a ninety minute match it was simply understood. So, we faced each other from the halves we had took when entering the field of play. Notwithstanding it was very good of them allowing us to kick-off as it meant we could start with the ball in our possession.

There is a saying in football, that it's a game of two halves, well in this game it was a game of two halves, with both halves being exactly the same, with the exception of the second half being curtailed shorter than full time as it eventually ended by itself when the vanquished team *en-masse* decided it was time to go with the opposition having the good grace of stopping play, but not done as a form of protest but done as it was time to call it quits due to the emphatic scoreline and general exhaustion.

At the start of the match, we were initially nervous or excited or whatever you may call it, which is normal, but it seemed worse here due to the circumstances however it faded, this fight or flight mode quickly adjusts to the reality of the situation and makes you forget everything because except being in the moment, So it was in this huge hubbub of noise surrounding us, we kicked off, Donny made a fatal mistake by not kicking off by allowing his fellow strike partner to do so, with a midfielder in the centre circle accepting his forward kick-off pass, whom then neatly passed the ball back to mid field and what turned out, was a nice move, a nice passage of play until the ball eventually went out of play. I remember one of the opposition players with no shoe's blast the ball full strength up-field over my head to a forward who narrowly got to it but his momentum meant he could only knocked the ball on but out for a throw in. The illusion I had of the opposition being at a handicap having in general no shoes was quickly dispelled after that, replaced by a sense of wonderment at how could you kick a ball, such a ball like that, with such strength.

After another very few short minutes we held our own and all at once there was a sense of feeling that we were in the game and confidence started to grow, it was helped in the very early stages by the crowd cheering anything positive we did and evaporated any feelings of intimidation from them, not that there was any. This made us feel we were in the game and with this new found belief, but as just mentioned this was a fleeting moment of perhaps five minutes or maybe even six!

In football matches, the game will either start at a rapid pace if one side is charged up or super confident and swarm all over the opposition, but in most games, it is more usual that a game will start at a moderate pace, until each side has weighed up the opposition and then adjust their play accordingly. This game was of the latter, starting moderately, but all this did was give us a false sense of security, because we couldn't really read them because we weren't very good, however in the initial stages exchanges we were doing all right, as nothing of note was happening with them, it seemed to me at that point, all we had to do is get the ball to Donny and he would do the rest.

During the initial exchanges of play, the ball broke down from one of their attacks and the ball was fizzed along the ground to me at pace by one of our defenders, with myself about 25m away from the goal with my back to it, it was a beautiful pass and at the corner of my eye I could see the Italian forward so as I ran towards the ball I hit it sweetly first time around the corner, (that was a first time)! Into the forwards path for him to run onto as it was just in front of him, for him then to control it, then pass it inside to Donny and for him to finish with aplomb 'bang 1-0'! But not in reality, as although it was passed to the Italian and travelling on the ground, the vision I had of him passing it back inside to Donny (he also had permed hair, but blonde), never materialised, as the Italian was surprised by the instant pass in front of him, almost like a goalie, when he gets rooted to the spot when a shot is fired at his goal and he has no chance of getting near it, so the Italian hesitated for a fraction until he realised where the pass was going and as he ran onto the pass, the ball passed him by, by a fraction and went out for a throw in. He did however acknowledge the pass.

Donny being Donny remonstrated with both of us like the *prima donna* he was. He made it look like it was something he'd seen many times that had stunted his career of becoming a centre forward of renown, that had never come to pass. There was I think, only one more attack from us if you could call it that, when our Italian forward stooped to put his head to the ball from a cross delivered from who knows who on our side! But it really was too low for a header, the defender could easily have kicked the ball away but would have had to kick our forwards head, so he didn't defend it, but this strike on goal as it turned out was like a back pass to their goalkeeper anyway.

Well, it must be said, that was about the full extent of us testing their goalkeeper, what with one being the previous ball going out for a throw-in plus the 'back pass'! Thereafter, I do not recall the ball ever being out of our half and after this initial spell, the oppositions shear tenacity, skill and at times bravery of heading a ball made of rock, but also kicking a ball made of rock in bare foot took its toll on us, slowly at first. Their first goal came after about ten minutes, then in quick succession they scored another couple. At this stage, we were chasing shadows, and all the while to a back drop of cheers from the home crowd.

At half time, half time wasn't signalled by a hooter or anything, it just happened as somebody on the pitch assumed it was half time, no spectator signalled it, so I suppose someone playing had to, you literally couldn't hear yourself think due to the noise around this pitch (which is still a fabulous memory). So, this fellow from the opposition bellowing out these words 'HALF TIME'! and half time it was!

I remember us going back to the shuttle buses and gulping half litre upon half litre bottles of water, to no avail at quenching the thirst. Nobody said a word as amongst us there was no leader to come to the fore, the closest we had to a leader was Donny, but I don't recall him ever actually touching the ball (not even in the warm up)!!!! So, no team talk, just a team of young guys with their heads all facing down, knowing that it was beyond doubt how inferior we were to the other side, words of any kind would not have made any difference anyways. After quenching our thirst as best we could, we went back through the crowd onto the pitch to our awaiting opponents, who were waiting to kick off as it was their turn, but we were in no hurry to continue to run around without the ball for the next half.

After this interlude, the game became a procession for the 'home' team, I remember seeing bits of skill on the ball I had never witnessed in real life before and with the swagger and confidence that comes with being about 7-0 up at the time. I think we only seemed to get the ball back into our possession after they had eventually decided to run forward and score another goal. This getting hold of the ball again was only gained by a re start and try as we did, just couldn't keep hold of the ball, every pass looked like we were trying to pass to our opponents, which we did at regular intervals, we just couldn't run, I think in retrospect we should have had substitutes, but really only so they could have experienced this occasion like we did. In one passage of play were with us outclassed, oh the irony, and a team completely out on its feet with fatigue, they should have been tired too, as we were much better fed that is for sure, and all young men, they kept the ball with some really clever little one-twos and triangles, but then didn't take a shot at goal, but rather, recycle the ball for a bit longer and then go up and score another goal. This was not showing boating, anyone who plays the game or knows the game can see that, but this was simply a love of playing, they simply wanted to keep the ball to do so, but at some point, they would eventually go up and try and score another goal. Again, it was not pre-scripted by any means but when the score got to 10-0. I think even though it didn't seem to be the full ninety minutes an un-collective decision was made ie by the white team only, to collect the ball and take it home, except of course we couldn't as it wasn't our ball. It was at this stage our opponents realised it was pointless in carrying on and they ended the game for us, to which we were thankful.

I know in most situations of defeat, this one was never really in doubt, there is usually a sense of disappointment of various degrees depending on one's countenance, usually followed by an inquisition to try and understand why it happened, but in this instance, there was no point in doing so, it was not even in anyone's thoughts, as no words can compensate or provide answers to how to be better next time when you're playing opponents that could beat you 101 times out of a 100.

When the game ended, our opponents warmly shook our hands with no sense of triumph, but rather in a sense of gratitude, and the crowd itself although ecstatic was also warm and appreciative of us as well and the sense of loss we felt became negligible, in fact I don't think any of us felt any sense of loss at all, all we felt was elation, afforded us by our hosts, and complete unbridled respect which we scarcely deserved, but their enthusiasm was beyond description and was infectious to the degree that made us delighted to be there, from prior to the apprehension we had felt going there.

Off course there was no changing rooms or showers to be had, I don't think they had showers, as I am almost certain they didn't, but can't be sure (but I am) from seeing the workers using hoses after a day's work when passing by in the shuttle bus on workdays. People came up to us all one on one or in small groups and spoke to us with enthusiasm and happiness, again it has to be said, not a sniff of gloating.

These *Aprè* match moments, they were wonderful, and as such these moments were the most memorable part of the day, because we had connected with people, people we never associated with in normal circumstances and felt as one, we had all shared in something that we all knew was a *Happening*, it truly was, and in many ways we didn't want to leave, but the reality also is, when your beaten, your beaten and its best to go. So, we all returned to the shuttle busses snaking through these grateful people. They as we were driven out of the compound, gazed upon us with smiling faces through the windows, not in triumph, but respect and gratitude and cheers, until eventually upon reaching the compound gates and onto the open road, as some of us looked back as did I, we witnessed the entire hut with scenes of people jumping and clapping and waving us off.

The two shuttle busses brought us back to the white hut, we all in my bus were silent, not because of the defeat, nor the sense of amazement that we had done this taboo thing, never heard tell of before, but because we were knackered and to talk would have been an effort, and besides we couldn't talk about how well we had played and talk about how we had scored this and that goal.

After it seemed about five minutes we were back in the white hut and the drivers let us out of the shuttle busses, we didn't have an inquest in the mess hall, we didn't do anything really, the site engineers got into their cars and the rest of us went back to our cells as I called them, even though they were classified as rooms.

Alone in my room, where it was OK to just collapse in tiredness. All I could ponder on in a positive way after such an experience, to bathe in the feelings of emotions of the thought that something had changed today, and it felt significant and a privilege of being involved in a *Happening* that it was without a doubt, because I felt it, something had changed in me and I could see on days after on site, the sense of superiority and the sense of inferiority had diminished, it had been replaced by an unconscious understanding and mutual respect, we certainly knew how skilled the workers were and what they could achieve and I think in turn the workers didn't appear to have a look of resentment that was an understandable look considering the circumstances.

What I had felt after the game was it seemed to me how everyone who was there felt. How could a football match do this? In reality it wasn't the football match, it was the reconciliation of different people without knowing that is what happened because of this game. So, it seems that communication is the key, as the saying goes when you're marching, you're not fighting, this goes just the same when by when you're talking, you're not fighting. As with all conflicts, conflicts of any kind, eventually after months, maybe years of sanctions, of wars, their comes a point when the only way resolution can be found is by actually communicating with the adversaries whether they are the aggressor or the victim in such conflicts of interest eventually the only real way to resolve a problem is to sit down and talk. Dialogue in which to reach a common ground and to allow resolution to be the outcome. I often think looking round at such world events, why don't they just sit down first and talk, because eventually that is what happens in the end. I slept well that night.

Chapter 10

10 -0

Firstly, we must acknowledge the people responsible for making the *Happening* happen and all the angst it released out of everyone who was there. What is good about football, is that it's colour blind. The object of the game is the same for everyone, football doesn't respect colour, the football, the primary object in the game doesn't even know what colour it is, so why would it matter what colour a person is when playing with such a thing? That is the same in all aspects of life of course.

The product of 10 times 0 is nothing

The ball of course is simply a metaphor for mankind. Just as the ball had no choice in what colour it was when it was created, neither did we.

What happened, happened, without people, without trust in trusting people we don't grow, to grow is based on a contract, and that contract is a contract of trust. We will never fulfil our full power without using the power of others, because collectively the power of others enhances our own powers, as you inherit theirs. Life doesn't owe you a living and for that matter you don't owe anyone else a living. It is up to you to earn a life and to earn a life is to live it and you can't live a life without others, otherwise you have no life, it really is that simple!!!

A man or a woman become better people, because inside all of us is an imperishable core that never diminishes, it gets clouded over by life events and to progress you must reach inside yourself no matter what and harness the you inside which although is not actually physical, it is real non the less, it is you that instructs your typewriter to write by using the appendages that are yours for a short time, these tools simply wear out and all that's left is you. This you that must reach out to others with the tools you have been given which are to be shared, as not to do so makes them meaningless.

But who is you? You are the innate entity which is invisible in these dimensions. Of all the dimensions we can understand there are only 4, these are of course: length, breath, height, time. (time is loosely defined as the 4th dimension), I chose not to put 'and' before time because dimensions don't end after the fourth dimension. As they are infinite, beyond our understanding. For instance: $10 \times 10 \times 10 = 1000^3$. Yet there is $10 \times 10 \times 10 \times 10 = 10000^4$. This is clearly 4 dimensional, but this fourth dimension is not in the same sense as time, as time is another dimension altogether! This particular fourth dimension is a real number, non the less. It's a dimension of another kind, I think, there lies nature of dimensions, they are beyond our understanding (yet) and as this simple analogy shows dimensions carry on infinitum.

People are not a body but use it as a mode of transport within this realm. Within other realms it is no use. Just like the black South Africans used their bodies to carry them through a subjugated regime and period but carried them it did. Until one day the dimensions of physical space and time outlasted a regime in which they were born into, it helped carry them through these times until these times no longer existed as this '4th' dimension outlasted Apartheid just like it does any other situations. We then use these same bodies to carry us through to the present, without the men in this case and countless others, perhaps unbeknown to themselves, as with all other women and men in other trying or unpalatable situations. They persevere, they persevere because they use other entities with a common purpose until one day we will realise we are all one, but before this happens we have a long way to go, until we are one in a realm where we will see ourselves as so, and that is why you must do all you can, with all you can and rely on other people in trust as they are you also, merely an extension of you in another form, to hurt anyone is to hurt yourself, you may not think it but eventually consciousness which again isn't physical, but guides you to this realisation, that you are simply hurting yourself.

You can laugh as you surely must at these words, but these words are written to try and make sense of it all, it is not to blaspheme it is to recognise what we are, we are all one we all belong to something we don't understand yet and that is why we must carry on until we escape the shackles of ourselves just like South Africans escaped the shackles of Apartheid which was shown in the people we played football with, and those who organised it, again with them not knowing by being kind to us, and kind they were, they were in fact being kind to themselves, because by being kind to others is to be kind to yourself.

Without this football match my mind or more precisely my consciousness would have remained dull and unenlightened, the bravery of these people has led to their freedom, freedom to join with all humankind as one. Without kindness we are nothing. We will be eventually be 1^n and quite a dimension that comes by being kind. So, all that is left now is to ask is: Do you want to be a 10 or do you want to be a 0?

It was the unbeknown foresight of these men
that is an example that by being respectful to
others, they were being respectful to themselves
and carried with them an integrity, that without
it, this ability to love, they would still be stuck in
that thing, that thing that was called Apartheid a
most ludicrous concept that was designed to
dissect our very selves, but was smashed apart
by kindness and oneness.

These actions of a few, understanding the needs
of others that created this *Happening*, created a
breakthrough moment, breaking down the myth
of any differences in humankind, it created a
culture of mutual respect and understanding that
was able to grow on this building site, the work
rate and construction difficulties were handled a
lot better after this. This is but a small acorn in
the grand scheme of things, but it was part of the
beginning of the end, simply by being kind. Kind
has its price, the price is bravery, the price is the
loss of lives of the many in the face of evil, but
their bravery and vision knew that eventually it
would break through tyranny as is the case, as it
will in all such places where there are conflicts of
this kind based on race or human rights, which
are usually the same.

The respect and gratitude given by people with so little just by being respected made them become what we must surely strive to be and that is kind. In such circumstances there is no alternative but courage which is only courage when there is risk, the risk to be kind. The primary purpose of life.

fin

Afterword

So, what did I learn? I learnt two things. The first thing I learned and have kept it with me ever since is we are all God's children, (as said by Isaac), which means to me nobody has the right to judge others as I don't have the right to judge anyone else without exception.

The second thing I learned, was to be of value in life you have to make yourself of value, not materialistically, although that would be nice, that is but transient. Being of value by being a servant to others in the sense of being of service by providing something positive of yourselves that it may be passed on, no matter how big no matter how small but to provide a positive aspect in what you do and how you treat others by giving due respect.

Printed in France by Amazon
Brétigny-sur-Orge, FR